19

October

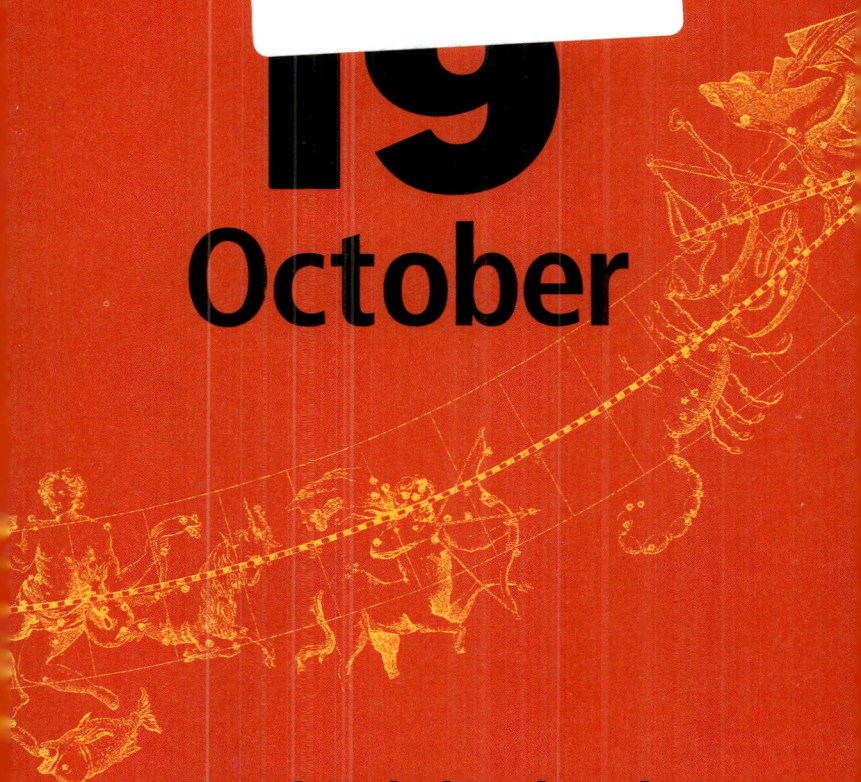

Your birthday book

Your genealogical tree

Great grandfather	Great grandmother	Great grandfather	Great grandmother
born:	*born:*	*born:*	*born:*

Grandmother

born:

Grandfather

born:

Mother

born:

You

born:

From the day you were born you became a part of your family's history. We have all wondered at one time or another about our 'roots'. What kind of people were my family? What did they do? Where they rich or poor? One way to find out about your ancestors is to trace your genealogy or 'family tree'. Genealogy is a fascinating pursuit and looking into your own, or anyone else's, can be like reading a good detective story. The first Greek writings were on ancestry while in the Bible there is a genealogy of the world's population from Adam and Eve onwards.

Today however, scarcely anyone can trace their family back further than the 11th century. But from the 1500s onwards people became enthralled by the subject.

Great grandfather

born:

Great grandmother

born:

Great grandfather

born:

Great grandmother

born:

Grandmother

born:

Grandfather

born:

Father

born:

Brother

born:

or Sister

born:

There are plenty of surviving manuscripts these days in local record offices. But the best way to begin finding out about your family is to start with yourself and work backwards, generation by generation. A good idea might be to talk to your parents and grandparents and other relatives. Valuable information may also be found in old diaries and letters. The further back you go the harder it will become. Who knows what you will find but be prepared: you may stumble upon a few skeletons in your family closet!

5

The calendars

Needing reliable reference points in time, ancient people began to observe the movements of the Sun, the Moon and the stars in order to establish cycles. Thus shepherds and navigators soon realised that they could use the sky as a clock and a calendar. Thanks to the Sun's regular progress around the Earth, men had a measure for time from very early on: daytime. Then by observing the return of the Sun to the same place on the Earth's horizon, they found another measure: the year, which corresponds with about 12 rotations of the Moon in the sky. The year was therefore divided up into 12 months, enough to lead to the introduction of a calendar which has ruled our lives for more than 4,000 years.

The Sun and the Moon follow different rhythms. Some people base their calendar on the Moon's

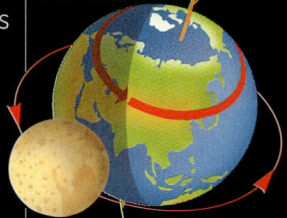

cycle and others on the Sun's. Whichever calendar we follow, its function is to give us the feeling that time is passing… and of course, no calendar, no birthday either…

The calendars

The Earth turns on its axis from east to west and travels around the Sun.

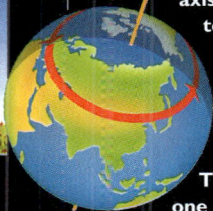

The Earth is one of the nine planets which revolve around a star, the Sun, and which together make up our solar system. The Sun is a burning ball of hot gases which is 100 times bigger than the Earth. It is just one star among the hundreds of millions which make up our galaxy, but it is the closest to the Earth.

The two hemispheres have opposite seasons.

The Earth takes 24 hours to turn on its axis: one day. The Moon, going through its phases (see opp. page) takes 29½ days to travel around the Earth: one lunar month. As for the Earth, it takes 365 days and

6 hours to travel around the Sun: one year. The solar year is split into 12 months and 11 days. The remaining days are added to the end of certain months: these have 31 days instead of 30.

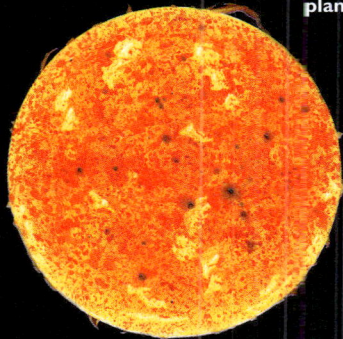

7

The Zodiac

The constellations of the Zodiac also gave people the means to combine their dreams with their observations and invent magical stories. Very soon astrologers were using the position of the planets in the Zodiac to predict the future. The planets and stars had a significance and secret meaning which influenced our moods, our character and our life. Astrology, the 'science of the stars', was Mankind's first attempt to understand his world.

From their observations of the sky, ancient people noticed that groups of stars, now called constellations, made shapes which they soon named. At first, these shapes helped to identify specific stars, allowing people to navigate the globe long before the invention of the compass. Then they realised that, seen from the Earth, the Sun, the Moon and the other planets traced a large circle in the sky which led them steadily back through the same constellations. As most of these were named after animals, this circle was called the Zodiac, a Greek word meaning 'circle of animals'. The Sun remains for one month in each constellation: where it was on your birthday determines your 'zodiacal sign'.

The Zodiac

ARIES: March 21 to April 20 ♈

TAURUS: April 21 to May 20 ♉

GEMINI: May 21 to June 22 ♊

CANCER: June 23 to July 22 ♋

LEO: July 23 to August 23 ♌

VIRGO: August 24 to September 23 ♍

LIBRA: September 24 to October 23 ♎

SCORPIO: October 24 to November 22 ♏

SAGITTARIUS: November 23 to December 21 ♐

CAPRICORN: December 22 to January 20 ♑

AQUARIUS: January 21 to February 19 ♒

PISCES: February 20 to March 20 ♓

The planets and their influence

Each of the planets has its own properties, just like the signs of the Zodiac on which they are thought to have a ruling influence. The planet Mars governs Aries, Pluto governs Scorpio; Venus governs Taurus and Libra; Saturn governs Capricorn, Mercury governs Virgo and Gemini; Jupiter governs Sagittarius; Neptune governs Pisces and Uranus governs Aquarius. The Sun, centre of our solar system and worshipped for thousands of years under many names, governs Leo – often called the 'Royal Sign' – and finally the Moon which governs the sign of Cancer.

Astrologers have always believed that the Sun, the Moon and the other planets of our solar sytem have a special relationship with one or more signs of the Zodiac, which adds to the subtle complexity of astrology. Not only do they think we are influenced by our zodiacal sign, but the relative positions of all the planets on the exact day and time of our birth is also thought to influence the kind of person we will grow up to be.

Neptune Uranus Saturn Jupiter Mars Earth Venus Mercury

We know that the Moon causes tides in the oceans, and that earthquakes have been attributed to its gravitational force. But from earliest times it was also thought to influence our moods: some people are indeed deeply affected by it – the word 'lunatic' comes from the belief that madness was caused by the phases of the Moon. Many myths grew up around it: in India it was believed that the Moon was the Sun's unfaithful bride, cut in two and only occasionally allowed to shine in her full beauty.

Our solar system, with the nine heavenly spheres.

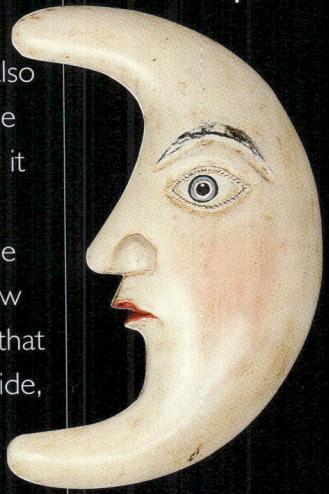

Your star sign – Libra

The Libra's motto is, not surprisingly, 'I weigh' and, indeed, weighing alternatives can be taken too far by them, which is why they are sometimes hesitant and indecisive. Their ability to see both sides of a question can prevent them from taking firm action and following it through.

Libra is the sign of balance. Its symbol, a pair of scales, evokes justice, measure and harmony in all things. The most sociable of all the signs, Librans are diplomatic, peace-loving and conciliatory by nature.

A highly aesthetic and sensuous sign ruled by Venus, Libra loves beauty in all its shapes and forms. Each sign is divided into three 'decans' or periods of ten days. These too have their characteristics. September 24–October 3 is Libra's first decan, October 4–13 is the second and October 14–23 is the third. Common to all three, however is the Libran's need to be in constant contact with other people in order to develop and fulfil his or her private destiny.

But at their best, Librans are kind, devoted, generous, charming and strongly believe that no one ought ever to be alone. They are unusually blessed with special physical grace, refinement and love of beauty. Each zodiacal sign is also associated with colours, plants, animals and so on thought to be beneficial. For Librans the colours are night blue, shocking pink and cherry red; their perfumes are jasmin and gardenia; their gemstone is the clear, blue sapphire; their flower is the violet and related animals are the horse, the dove and the salmon. The Libran's special day is Friday.

The stars of your decan

The third decan of Libra is traditionally associated with the constellation Corona Borealis, the Northern Cross. Those born in this decan can weave a spell over their audience: they are the eloquent charmers. **Chuck Berry** (Oct. 18, 1926), the rock 'n' roll pioneer, and **Franz Liszt** (Oct. 22, 1811, right), the Hungarian composer and piano virtuoso who invented the 'piano recital', are the music-makers of your decan. **Pierre Larousse** (Oct. 23, 1817, above right), who said he wanted to 'teach everyone about everything', accomplished his aim by publishing a comprehensive dictionary which is of lasting value. Also filed under research in your decan is **Noah Webster** (Oct. 16, 1758, below), the American lexicographer who with his dictionary gave American English respectability and vitality. Other men of words include the Roman master of poetry **Virgil** (Oct. 15, AD 70), the German philosopher **Friedrich Nietzsche** (Oct. 15, 1844), the witty and flamboyant Irish writer **Oscar Wilde** (Oct. 16, 1854), author of *The Portrait of Dorian Gray*;

couturier **Ralph Lauren** (Oct. 14, 1939), who put chic into casual with his 'Polo' range; science fiction author and film director **Michael Crichton** (Oct. 23, 1942), whose story

Robbins (Oct. 16, 1958). Finally there are two sporting icons: tennis pro **Martina Navratilova** (Oct. 18, 1956), nine times winner of the Wimbledon Women's Singles title, and the

the romantic **Arthur Rimbaud** (Oct. 20, 1854, right), who abandoned writing at the age of 19, and **Italo Calvino** (Oct. 15, 1923), the Italian master of the fable whose whimsical stories have given contemporary literature a playful twist. Other creative people in your decan include **Hokusai** (Oct. 21, 1760), the Japanese master artist whose beautiful waves and views of Mount Fuji are world famous; **Sir Christopher Wren** (Oct. 20, 1632), architect of St Paul's Cathedral; American

Jurassic Park made him a household name; and Hollywood stars **Rita Hayworth** (Oct. 17, 1918), perhaps best remembered in Charles Vidor's *Gilda* (1946), and **Tim**

Brazilian footballer **Edson Arantes do Nascimento**, otherwise known as Pele (Oct. 23, 1940), who made the No. 10 shirt his own as the greatest football player in the world.

Star of the day

Even before the arrival in France of Thomas Edison's 'Kinetoscope' Auguste (left) and Louis (right) had already made improvements in photographic technique. When Edison's wonderful new gadget took the French public by storm, the brothers turned their attention to motion pictures.

In 1894 they perfected their 'cinématographe', an instrument which combined camera, printer and projector, and exhibited it at the Grand Café in Paris on December 28. One of the greatest advances of their machine was the introduction of perforations on the film, which ensured a regular unravelling of the celluloid tape and thus a smooth and realistic image. The Lumière brothers then sent cameramen throughout the world to make the

Auguste Lumière, one of the earliest pioneers of the cinema, was born in France today in 1862. Without Auguste and his brother Louis, the cinema as we know it today would not exist. They perfected existing technologies, combining the inventions and discoveries of others to achieve something altogether new.

first animated records of important events. The Lumière brothers went on to conduct some of the earliest successful experiments in large screen, stereoscopic and colour film systems.

CINÉMATOGRAPHE LUMIÈRE

Today

The **Autogiro** (right), a primitive form of helicopter, underwent its first tests in Farnborough, England, today in 1925. Heavier than an aircraft, the Autogiro supported itself with a rotary wing which provided lift but not propulsion. Thus the craft could go up but then could do nothing but come down again. It was soon to be

superseded by the helicopter.

A rather more successful flier, the Handly Page Hampstead (opp. page, top), was delivered to Imperial Airways today in 1925.

The first three-engined airliner, the Handly had Jaguar engines mounted, one on each wing and one on its nose.

During the latter stages of the American War of Independence, the British forces led by Lord Cornwallis surrendered, bringing to an end the **Siege of Yorktown** today in 1781. The American troops under George Washington celebrated with a procession of banners through the streets, realising that, after five years of fighting, the British

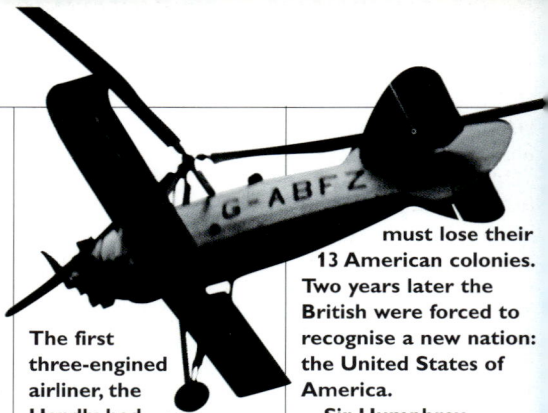

must lose their 13 American colonies. Two years later the British were forced to recognise a new nation: the United States of America.

Sir Humphrey Davy announced the discovery of **sodium** (Na) today in 1807.

Only a month after

Na

reaching Moscow **Napoleon Bonaparte** withdrew his weary army back towards France in 1812. Though he had lost 30,000 men in taking the Russian capital he lost many more in the retreat, faced with an even deadlier enemy: the Russian winter. Of the original 600,000 troops

Napoleon had taken only 100,000 survived.

Charles Ulm (below) landed in Australia today in 1933, 6 days and 17 hours after taking off from Britain. The previous record of 7 days and 5 hours had been set by Charles Kingsford Smith who died in 1934 while attempting to break Ulm's new record.

Ludwig van Beethoven's **Unfinished Symphony** received its world première today in 1988, or 161 years after his death.

The 'Great Mogul', as Haydn had nicknamed him, died during a thunderstorm in March 1827 before he was able to complete what would have been his 11th symphonic work.

'I cannot but conclude the bulk of your natives to be the most pernicious race of little odious vermin that nature ever suffered to crawl upon the surface of the earth.' Such was the verdict on mankind of **Jonathan Swift**, the Irish satirist and author of *Gulliver's Travels*, who died today in 1745.

Event of the day

PULLMAN

George Pullman, the US industrialist and inventor of the Pullman sleeping-car, died today in 1897. It was in 1853, while travelling across America selling his brother's furniture, that he first hit on the idea of a sleeping-car during a night-time journey from Buffalo to Westfield. Seated on a wooden bench, with no light, heating or toilets; unable to get a moment of sleep, it suddenly struck him that there had to be a better way to travel by rail at night.

It was another ten years before Pullman, together with an associate, Ben Field, could find the funds to build a prototype sleeping carriage. At a cost of $20,000 the two of them designed the 'Pioneer' in 1863. It was a disaster. It was too high, too wide and banged against the platform when they tried to put it on the rails. It was also very heavy and once they did get it on the tracks the 'Pioneer' proved too much for the steam-powered engine to pull. This

Death of George Pullman

luxury sleeping-car? The authorities agreed and on May 2, 1865 Lincoln's body was moved by rail to Springfield, Kentucky. Two years later Pullman had 48 sleeping-cars (for live travellers!) and a huge factory, the first planned industrial town in all of America.

might have been the end for Pullman had it not been for President Abraham Lincoln's assassination in 1865. The President's body had to be brought back from Washington for burial in his native state of Kentucky. How better to take the American hero home than in a

Inventions of the month

Every month, if not every year, sees its own share of inventions, great or otherwise, which shape our everyday lives. October is no exception.

A new style of calendar, known as the **Gregorian Calendar**, after its creator, Pope Gregory XIV, came into existence on October 4, 1582. It replaced the old Julian calendar, created in 44 BC by the Roman general Julius Caesar. The Julian calendar, with its year of 365.25 days was too long by some 11 minutes 14 seconds. This error became measurable in days over the centuries so in 1582 Pope Gregory ruled that October 5 should be called October 15. This change took place immediately in Italy, France, Spain and Portugal, but the new-style calendar was not used in England and its colonies until 1752.

On certainly more entertaining note October 21, 1848 saw an invention of a very different sort: the **can-can**, a dance that delighted audiences at the Paris dance halls where – with much high-kicking and swirling of petticoats – it was performed. No one knows where the name comes from, although one meaning of the word in French is 'quacking like a duck'.

On October 21, 1879 Thomas Edison wrote in his journal, 'Today the sight we had so long desired to see met our eyes.' It was the trial of 'No 9' – a bulb, exhausted of air, with a carbon filament lit by electricity – a **light bulb**!

'What a beautiful thing to have invented', said one of his excited technicians as they sat up all night staring at the light. It burnt for over 13 hours before the glass broke. 'If it can burn that number of hours,' said Edison, 'I know I can make it burn hundred.'

Tobacco heir Griswold Lorillard shocked fellow guests at that year's ultra-fashionable ball at the country club at Tuxedo Park, New York, when on October 10, 1886 he turned up in a brand new fashion style: a dress coat, but without the usual 'tails'. The short jacket, which was promptly named **tuxedo** in honour of its first appearance, went on to oust the old tails and to become what Britain calls a 'dinner jacket'.

The world's first **matches** were patented by Alonzo Phillips of Massachusetts on October 24, 1836. Unlike today's safety matches, these were much cruder affairs. A piece of wood soaked in sulphur was dragged against sand-paper, thus producing a flame. Book matches, used around the world for advertising and information, were invented in 1892.

Finally, the first **spring mattress** was patented by Samuel Pratt on October 18, 1826.

The seasons

Autumn, for the English poet John Keats the 'Season of mists and mellow fruitfulness', is also a period of change. Life in the Northern Hemisphere starts to move slowly: migratory birds gather in the trees and line up on telegraph poles before setting out on their long journey to warmer climates, while plants and animals begin to adapt themselves in preparation for the coming winter.

The migration of the crane, flying by day and night, is a spectacular sight. Flying in large groups, usually in a V- or W-shaped formation, they advance slowly and gracefully, filling the air with their mournful and disturbing cries. They can cover huge distances, stopping only to feed in favourite resting places. To the Japanese the crane is a symbol of wisdom. During its winter

courtship the crane's elaborate display reveals its striking black-and-white plumage against the snow, and has inspired many Japanese artists. The monarch butterfly is another marathon migrator. Before winter sets in it travels over 3,000 miles from Canada in the north to the sunnier climes

of southern Mexico, drifting on the air currents in search of its main source of nourishment – the milkweed. Late autumn comes and the days draw in and as the light fades leaves fall to the ground, giving the trees a better chance of surviving the cold weather. Chlorophyll, the green pigment which allows plants to

replenish the food in their leaves, is no longer produced. Red and brown pigments now appear and give the trees their rich autumnal hues. The sap can no longer reach the leaves and they die so that the tree may live. Fir trees do not lose their needles as these are smaller and can resist both the cold and lack of light. This is why they are 'ever green'.

Festivals of the month

'Roll out the barrel!' is the cry of beer-loving punters everywhere as they head for Munich's 16-day **Oktoberfest** (Oct. 21, right). The feast begins with parades of decorated beer wagons and people dressed in folk costumes, right down to the much-mentioned lederhosen. The Lord Mayor of the city has the privilege of opening the first barrel, whereupon the serious boozing commences. By contrast, Phuket in Thailand observes a nine-day **Vegetarian Festival** (late Sep. or Oct.), during which devout Taoists abstain from meat. This is accompanied by mind-boggling feats of mortification – walking on hot coals, skewering of cheeks and tongues, and hanging from hooks dug into the skin. **Hallowe'en** (Oct. 31), with its ghouls and trick-or-treating youngsters, seems tame by comparison.

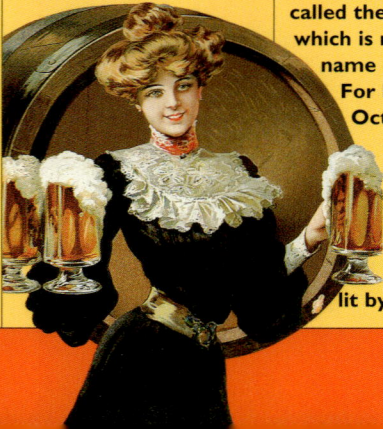

Eskimos celebrate the Festival of the **Bearded Seal** in October; a time for hunters to revere the souls of the hunted. A harpoon, in which the seal's soul is thought to reside, is stood by a lamp during the first night. No work is permitted for three days, after which the bladders of all the bearded seals caught in the past year are sunk through a hole in the ice. Jews embark on a seven-day harvest festival originally called the **Feast of the Ingathering** (above left). Meals are eaten in a trellis-roofed hut called the 'sukkot', which is now also the name of the festival. For Buddhists October is a time of great joy as the Buddha returns from heaven in the **Festival of Light**, his way lit by fire-balloons,

lanterns and candles. Hindus in India honour the fierce goddess Durga, the vanquisher of demons: **Durga Puja** (Sep.–Oct.) involves nine days of prayer and nine nights of dancing when all dress up.

In Morocco there are **Fantasias** (Oct. 7, left) celebrating the mighty Arab horses which take part in a spectacular charges through the cities. The most spectacular fantasia is to be seen in the city of Meknes. Finally in Australia, the town of Bowral greets the spring with a **Tulip**

Festival, with over 60,000 blooms spreading a blaze of colour through parks and gardens.

National event of the month

King Henry V of England, in his bid to capture the French throne, led the English into battle at Agincourt in northern France on the morning of October 25, 1415. Henry's army numbered only 12,000 and faced a French force nearly four times that. Yet at the end of the day the French had lost 5,000 men with a further 1,000 taken prisoner while the rest had fled. The victorious English army had lost a mere 1,000.

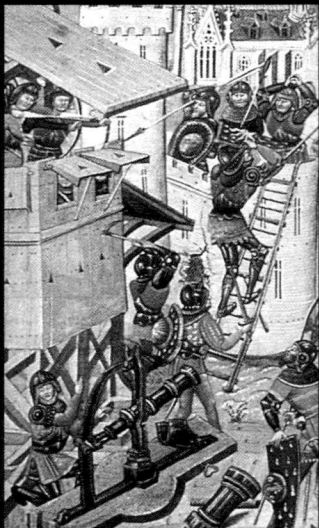

The Battle of Agincourt

The night before the battle it had rained non-stop and both armies had a long, wet wait. The English army was well disciplined, while the French were in jubilant mood, assuming that they would easily win the battle. But as they began their advance they found themselves bogged down in the cloying mud. Three times they attacked and three times they were repulsed. Then, they took flight as arrows were raining down on them. Seeing the enemy in retreat, the English archers threw away their bows and pushed forward, striking down and killing without mercy until the the French were in tatters. The battle lasted until 4 o'clock when the French were finally overwhelmed. In this way Henry won northern France and in 1420 he was made heir to the French throne. Sadly for him, he died before being crowned but his son, Henry VI, was made King of France in 1431.

Last words...

'I think, therefore I am,' wrote the French philosopher René Descartes. *Here are some of the thoughts people have had today.*

1745

I am what I am. I am what I am. (last words)
Jonathon Swift (1667-1745) *Irish satirist*

1818

My dearest Albert came to me...I told him I felt so grateful to him and would do everything to make him happy. I gave him a ring with the date of the ever dear to me 15th engraved in it. I also gave him a little seal I used to wear. I asked if he would let me have a little of his dear hair.
Queen Victoria (1819-1901) *English monarch*

1937

Well; I will go to Maples about the chaircovers; to Highgate to see Roger's house; & dream today, because I must unscrew my head & somehow freshen up if I am to write, to live, to go through the next lap with zest, not like old sea weed.
Virginia Woolf (1882-1941) *English writer*

1971

You cannot shake hands with a clenched fist.
Indira Gandhi (1917-84) *Indian stateswoman*